# Lions and Donkeys

A play

Steve Harper

Samuel French — London
www.samuelfrench-london.co.uk

© 2009 BY STEVE HARPER

Rights of Performance by Amateurs are controlled by Samuel French Ltd, 52 Fitzroy Street, London W1T 5JR, and they, or their authorized agents, issue licences to amateurs on payment of a fee. **It is an infringement of the Copyright to give any performance or public reading of the play before the fee has been paid and the licence issued.**

The Royalty Fee indicated below is subject to contract and subject to variation at the sole discretion of Samuel French Ltd.

Basic fee for each and every
performance by amateurs     Code D
in the British Isles

---

**The publication of this play does not imply that it is necessarily available for performance by amateurs or professionals, either in the British Isles or Overseas. Amateurs and professionals considering a production are strongly advised in their own interests to apply to the appropriate agents for written consent before starting rehearsals or booking a theatre or hall.**

---

ISBN 978 0 573 14213 0

The right of Steve Harper to be identified as author
of this work has been asserted by him in accordance with
Section 77 of the Copyright, Designs and Patents Act 1988.
Please see page iv for further copyright information

## LIONS AND DONKEYS

First presented at the Hunstanton Drama Festival in June 2009 with the following cast:

| | |
|---|---|
| **Corporal David Rawlings** | Jonathon Rice |
| **Sergeant Thomas Atkins** | Peter Duhig |
| **Lieutenant Harry Hargreaves** | Andy Mussell |
| **Lieutenant Willy Schmitt** | Richard Abel |

Produced and directed by Steve Harper

COPYRIGHT INFORMATION
(See also page ii)

This play is fully protected under the Copyright Laws of the British Commonwealth of Nations, the United States of America and all countries of the Berne and Universal Copyright Conventions.

All rights, including Stage, Motion Picture, Radio, Television, Public Reading, and Translation into Foreign Languages, are strictly reserved.

**No part of this publication may lawfully be reproduced in ANY form or by any means — photocopying, typescript, recording (including video-recording), manuscript, electronic, mechanical, or otherwise — or be transmitted or stored in a retrieval system, without prior permission.**

Licences are issued subject to the understanding that it shall be made clear in all advertising matter that the audience will witness an amateur performance; that the names of the authors of the plays shall be included on all announcements and on all programmes; and that the integrity of the authors' work will be preserved.

The Royalty Fee is subject to contract and subject to variation at the sole discretion of Samuel French Ltd.

In Theatres or Halls seating Four Hundred or more the fee will be subject to negotiation.

In Territories Overseas the fee quoted in this Acting Edition may not apply. A fee will be quoted on application to our local authorized agent, or if there is no such agent, on application to Samuel French Ltd, London.

---

VIDEO-RECORDING OF AMATEUR PRODUCTIONS

Please note that the copyright laws governing video-recording are extremely complex and that it should not be assumed that any play may be video-recorded for *whatever purpose* without first obtaining the permission of the appropriate agents. The fact that a play is published by Samuel French Ltd does not indicate that video rights are available or that Samuel French Ltd controls such rights.

## CHARACTERS

**Corporal David Rawlings**, early 20s, member of the British Army
**Sergeant Thomas Atkins**, late 20s, member of the British Army
**Lieutenant Harry Hargreaves**, 20, officer in the British Army.
**Lieutenant Willy Schmitt**, late 20s, officer in the German Army.

The action takes place on the Western Front, Observation Point 435.

Time—September 1918

# LIONS AND DONKEYS

*The setting is a British dugout on the Western Front, Observation Point 435 for the Third Essex Battallion. There is a simple table and two chairs. The table is set with a field phone, three tin mugs, some papers, an ashtray, a box of Swan Vesta matches and a packet of Woodbines. A map is pinned on a wall next to a duty list with many names crossed off, and a saucy picture of a 1918 starlet*

*The* CURTAIN *rises as music from "It's a Long Way to Tipperary" fades*

*Corporal Rawlings enters with two mugs of tea*

**Rawlings**  Cup of tea, Sarnt, come and get it while it's hot. Come on, you bugger, where are you? Oh well. (*Seeing the packet of Woodbines on the table*) Oily Rag, Corporal Rawlings? Most kind, don't mind if I do. (*He lights a cigarette, sits down and relaxes*)

*Sergeant Atkins enters and sees Rawlings*

**Atkins**  On your feet, you horrible man. Just look at you — your bleedin' mother wouldn't forgive you if she saw what you've done to that uniform. You're a disgrace to the British Army. What are you? Consider yourself on a charge.
**Rawlings**  (*getting up*) Yes, Sarnt. Will I be shot at dawn, Sarnt?
**Atkins**  Take any more of my fags, and I'll bloody shoot you myself.
**Rawlings**  You can't do that, Sarnt. Not without a full court-martial.
**Atkins**  Don't tell me,
**Rawlings** }
**Atkins**      (*together*) Says so in King's Regulations.
**Atkins**  (*helping himself to a Woodbine*) Can I bayonet you?

**Rawlings** Not if I give you this cup of cha.
**Atkins** Fair enough. Any messages from HQ?
**Rawlings** Only the usual request for enemy body counts, and a warning that the barrage starts at twenty-three thirty sharp. We're on a night attack again.
**Atkins** You did give them the co-ordinates, and range…
**Rawlings** Course I did, you think I want to go the same way as Jones, Bradley and the other poor sods?
**Atkins** Right, and have you let our friends know?
**Rawlings** Yes, no reciprocal arrangements tonight.
**Atkins** Right, so it's all peace and quiet until Jerry advances.
**Rawlings** I'm expecting the Bosch night party at about twenty-three hundred.
**Atkins** All set?
**Rawlings** Yes, the boys know what to expect — Sarge?
**Atkins** What?
**Rawlings** Do you really think it's nearly over?
**Atkins** Well, that's what they're all saying. But I seem to remember it was all going to be over by Christmas four years ago.
**Rawlings** Jesus, is it four years now? There can't be many of us left that have been here from the kick-off. Wipers, Passion Dale, Ver Dun. Christ, Tom, how many do you think have died?
**Atkins** Too many, Dave, too many.
**Rawlings** I wonder why we've been the lucky ones. Well I know we've both had our fair share of wounds, never a Blighty one though. But look at you, somebody up there is looking out for you, Mr Tommy bloody Atkins, coming back from the dead.
**Atkins** My father liked Kipling; thought it was funny to call me Thomas back in 1892.
**Rawlings** What?
**Atkins** Never mind.

*Sounds of movement can be heard offstage. Atkins pauses, listening*

What's that?
**Rawlings** Dunno, Sarge.

**Atkins** Well go and look, man!

*Rawlings exits for a moment, then rushes back in*

**Rawlings** Oh my good God, Tom, it's only a bloody officer!
**Atkins** Shit, they didn't send any message.

*Rawlings checks the field phone*

**Rawlings** Dead, the wire must have been hit again.
**Atkins** Right, keep calm, let's have him in here, and follow my lead.

*Rawlings sits and puts his head in his hands*

**Rawlings** Oh Jesus, Mary and Joseph, we've bloody had it! What are we going to do, Tom, what are we going to do?
**Atkins** On your feet, Corporal Rawlings, ATTENTION! We've come through too much to lose it now. We are the survivors of the Third Essex's front line observation point. We are the last of the few. We are bloody bulletproof —
**Rawlings** }
**Atkins** } (*together*) Says so in King's Regulations.
**Atkins** Right, get him in here now, we've only got fifteen minutes before we reckon Jerry will be over the top.
**Rawlings** Sarnt.

*Rawlings exits. He returns a moment later with Lieutenant Hargreaves*

*Atkins stands to attention*

**Hargreaves** Stand easy, Sergeant.
**Atkins** Sir.
**Hargreaves** I expect you're wondering why I'm here tonight, Sergeant.
**Atkins** Been a while since we've had an officer up here with us, sir. Nobody with you, sir?

**Hargreaves** No. I'm afraid a whizz bang got a little too close in the main line and Private Stanley died of wounds less than an hour ago. He was my batman, and a fine fellow. (*To Cpl Rawlings*) Sufficient firewood up here, Corporal?

**Rawlings** Er — yes, sir, thank you, sir.

**Hargreaves** Well be a bloody hero and heat up some tea with some of it would you, there's a good chap. One sugar please. Oh and you'd better get the sergeant a cup too.

**Rawlings** Sir.

*Rawlings exits*

**Hargreaves** It is Sergeant Atkins, isn't it?

**Atkins** Sir.

**Hargreaves** Is it really "Tommy Atkins"?

**Atkins** It is, sir.

**Hargreaves** Did you know that Rudyard Kipling had written a poem about you?

**Atkins** About me, sir? No, sir.

**Hargreaves** Well not about you personally Sergeant, but then I don't suppose you did a lot of English Literature at school.

**Atkins** No, sir.

**Hargreaves** Ah well, there we have it I suppose. I rather liked Kipling — would have been part of my course at Cambridge. But then that doesn't count for too much out here, does it?

**Atkins** If you say so, sir.

**Hargreaves** But we digress, Sergeant. I was telling you why I have risked life and limb to journey to the most forward position in the whole of the front line. It is to see you, Sergeant.

**Atkins** Me, sir?

**Hargreaves** Yes, Sergeant, I have a message for you from Field Marshal Haig.

**Atkins** For me, sir?

**Hargreaves** Yes, sir, for you, sir. Well not directly from the old man himself, but certainly from the general staff. (*He produces a letter. Reading*) "Sergeant Thomas Atkins of His Majesty's Third Essex Battalion. In recognition of outstanding courage and leadership whilst being in sole command of Forward Observation Point Number 435 on the Western Front, and while facing prolonged attack from superior enemy strength for over four weeks, you are to be awarded the Military Medal." It goes on a bit about how the enemy losses have been considerable, and ours minimal. Blah de blah... and how you never even thought of abdicating responsibility by asking for an officer to replace Captain Jennings after he was killed ... etc., etc. Well, there we have it, signed with the grateful thanks of Lord Haig, or at least one of his adjutants. How does that feel, Sergeant Atkins MM?

**Atkins** Permission to sit down, sir?

**Hargreaves** Of course, old man, and may I be the first to offer my congratulations. (*He shakes Atkins' hand*)

*Rawlings enters with two mugs of tea*

*Atkins sits, looking dazed*

**Rawlings** Excuse me, sir, but here's your tea and one for the sarnt. I took the liberty of putting a little drop of rum in, sir, to ward off the cold for your journey.

**Hargreaves** Journey, Corporal?

**Rawlings** Oh yes, sir, gets a bit hairy round here soon. Expecting another big push from Fritz, sir. Begging pardon, sir, is Sarnt Atkins all right? He's gone a bit pale, sir.

**Hargreaves** Sergeant Atkins has just received news of a long overdue recognition. He is to be awarded the Military Medal. And if this post is under imminent attack then I rather think I should be inspecting the men. A few words of encouragement from an officer can mean a lot, Corporal, you should know that.

**Atkins** No, sir, the Corporal's right, this is no place for you, sir. We're old hands at this. The boys and me will be fine, sir. Best thing you can do is report back to HQ, and tell them all's well at 435 and we're proud to be fighting for King and country, sir. The wire's down again I'm afraid, but I can send Corporal Rawlings to escort you back to the main line, sir. Bit of a shock about the medal, sir, just not sure I deserve it.

**Hargreaves** Sergeant Atkins, they do not hand MMs out with the bully beef. If you received it, you deserved it, understand?
**Atkins** Sir.
**Hargreaves** I might be the new boy out here, and you're probably thinking that I'm younger than most of the men, but I shall not run from a fight. If the Huns are attacking, then I presume you will need every last rifle you can muster. I'm not doubting the leadership of a man that holds the Military Medal, I'm just here to do my duty. Is that clear, Sergeant?
**Rawlings** (*sotto voce*) Oh bloody hell.
**Atkins** Shut it, Corporal. Yes, sir, that's clear, sir.
**Hargreaves** Good, now perhaps you would introduce me to some of the men.

*The sound of singing (a lewd music hall song) can be heard off stage*

Ah, who's this?

*Lieutenant Schmitt enters with a bottle and a large sausage*

**Schmitt** Tommy, Tommy, I have something special for you tonight.
**Hargreaves** What in God's name?
**Atkins** Ah, sir, yes, allow me to introduce — ah —
**Rawlings** Lieutenant Schmitt of the — Free Icelandic Army, sir.
**Atkins** (*sotto voce*) Oh God.
**Hargreaves** I'm sorry, did you say the Free Icelandic Army?
**Schmitt** *Ja*, er — yes Loitnant. I too am Loitnant. Willy Smith of the er — Glacier Division Icelandic Free Troops.
**Hargreaves** Good God, I didn't even know your lot were over here. (*He shakes hands*) Lieutenant Harry Hargreaves, Third Essex.
**Schmitt** Ah, yes I am afraid Lord Kitchener has kept very quiet about Iceland's role. We are a bit of the political embarrassment; how do you say, too little too late. Still we are here now. Which is jolly good as tonight I have brought *wurst*. Ah, sausage.
**Hargreaves** Your uniform is a little puzzling, Lieutenant.
**Atkins** (*sotto voce*) Gordon Bennett!

**Schmitt**  Again the great embarrassment, Iceland uniforms they are white for the snows of the homeland, but here is not good colour for the snipers. So on Western Front we borrow from our friends and allies. When they have no more need. (*He puts his finger through a bullet hole*) Soon new uniforms will arrive.

**Hargreaves**  I see. Sergeant Atkins, I believe you said there were no officers at this observation station?

**Schmitt**  That is correct, Harry, although I am Loitnant in Free Icelandic force, I am still waiting for confirmation that my old rank is accepted by new allies. A mere formality, but Sergeant Atkins is quite correct, officially I hold no rank in the British army.

**Hargreaves**  This all sounds most irregular. I think I shall need to report what is going on here.

**Rawlings**  No need for that, sir, the Brass will be well aware of the problems of inter, er, inter ——

**Atkins**  Integrating

**Rawlings**  Yeah, integrating foreign troops into His Majesty's army, sir. I mean look at the Anzacs.

**Atkins**  The Sepoys.

**Schmitt**  The Americans.

**Hargreaves**  Yes, but I'm pretty damn sure they all came with the proper uniform. I mean good Lord, for all I know you could be German.

**Rawlings**  That's very good, sir, German, yes, nice to have an officer with a bit of humour, in these dark times, sir.

**Hargreaves**  No I'm sorry, Lieutenant, this just will not do. May I see your papers?

**Schmitt**  Papers?

**Hargreaves**  Yes, man, your orders, pay book, Icelandic commission.

**Schmitt**  Ah. Sadly lost under fire.

**Atkins**  Look, sir, if I vouch for Lieutenant Schmitt, would that be in order, sir? He saved my life, sir. I would be long dead if it hadn't been for him, sir. Everything is all right, sir, honestly.

**Hargreaves**  The devil it is. There's something going on here, and you, Sergeant, are going to tell me exactly what it is.

**Rawlings**  Or what?

**Hargreaves**  What did you say, Corporal?

**Rawlings** I said, "or what?" You stroll in here after a couple of days up at the Front and think you can get us all shot. Well let me tell you, cocker, the Kaiser, the Brass and His Majesty's bloody artillery have been trying for the past four years. What makes you think you can do it when they can't? ... Sir.

**Atkins** That's enough, Corporal.

**Hargreaves** Yes that is enough, Corporal. Sergeant, put this man on a charge, gross insubordination.

**Rawlings** Tommy.

**Schmitt** Oh dear, I am afraid I am the cause of all this problem. I think I arrive a little too early. I am so sorry, Harry, but I must ask you to hand over your revolver. (*He produces his own gun*)

**Hargreaves** What the devil?

**Schmitt** Allow me to re-introduce myself, Harry. I am Oberloitnant Vilhelm Von-Schmitt of the Imperial German Army. I really have no desire to kill you, but considering you have probably ruined a perfectly good social evening, and taking into account we are at war, I hope you will appreciate the gravity of your situation.

**Hargreaves** This can't be happening.

**Atkins** Oh I'm afraid it can, sir.

**Rawlings** Why don't we just shoot him? We could say a sniper got him. Never did like officers.

**Schmitt** Does that include me, David? And no, I think we have all seen enough pointless death to last a lifetime. Your pistol please, Harry.

*Hargreaves reluctantly hands over his gun*

**Atkins** I suppose we owe you an explanation, sir.

**Hargreaves** You'll all be shot for this, you know that don't you? Now look, Sergeant, I'm offering you a last chance. Shoot that Hun and arrest Corporal Rawlings and I'll speak up for you at the court martial. You're a holder of the Military Medal for God's sake.

**Atkins** I'm afraid it doesn't work like that up here, sir. King's Regulations are more likely to get you killed than the Kaiser's mob. We've sort of got a private arrangement at Observation Point 435. Perhaps I should go back to the start and tell you why.

**Schmitt** I'm going to put my gun away now, Harry. Please do not do anything stupid. Perhaps you would do us the courtesy of listening to Sergeant Atkins. It is at the very least an interesting story. (*He puts his gun away*)

**Hargreaves** Am I to be killed?

**Schmitt** No, Harry, there is no reason for you to die.

**Hargreaves** Very well. Treason is a serious business. I'd be interested to see how you are going to talk your way out of it. Or will you let Lieutenant Schmitt do the talking for you? His English seems an improvement on Corporal Rawlings'.

**Rawlings** Oh bloody hell, Willy, just shoot him.

**Schmitt** No. Thank you for the compliment, Harry. Like Bismarck I too have English relations. I have spent holidays at Maidstone. May I ask how old you are, Harry?

**Hargreaves** Name, rank and number is all you'll get out of me.

**Schmitt** Very well, I would think you are no more than nineteen.

**Hargreaves** Twenty.

**Schmitt** So. Tommy, David and myself have been fighting this war since you were sixteen. We have seen horrors that no man should have to witness. Battalions scythed down by machine guns like summer corn. Men coughing their lungs up with chlorine gas. Younger soldiers than you left to die screaming on the wire. Colleagues drowning in mud, rats eating those not quite dead.

**Rawlings** Mates blown to pieces in front of you, so you have to wipe their brains off of your face.

**Atkins** Men burnt until they look like black sticks with the screams still on their faces.

**Rawlings** The lice, the cold, lack of rations, shitting yourself when the heavy bombardment starts

**Schmitt** Not the glory they promised us back at home is it, Harry? How did your *Times* newspaper put it? Ah yes, lions led by donkeys.

**Atkins** I know this looks bad, sir, but things just happened this way.

**Hargreaves** Go on.

**Atkins** About five weeks ago we got orders, there would be a heavy bombardment of the German lines. Artillery was to bombard them with 88s and mortars. Then at four o'clock we were over the top and to advance on the enemy line. Captain Jennings was at the end of his tether, poor sod, he was drunk by midnight. Well, a lot of us was. At three fifty-five the guns stopped and the Captain blew his whistle. Forty-seven of us from station 435 started out. We had only got about forty yards past our wire when the bloody artillery started up again. Confusion in the chain of command, they said. I was about twenty feet behind Captain Jennings when a moaning minney landed short. It blew me thirty feet into another shell crater together with Captain Jennings' left leg. That was all that was left of him.

**Schmitt** We too had received orders for the same night. We were to go into no-man's-land and try to capture men from isolated units for interrogation. Eight members of my patrol started out at two o'clock, and then we found ourselves pinned down by artillery. Weiner, Gloss and Vinkler were killed by the barrage. So we decided to move towards your lines. There seemed to be less chance of being shot than being blown to kingdom come. We did not count on the artillery pattern following us. In the confusion I was separated from my men. I received a shrapnel wound to the shoulder and crawled into a shell hole to take cover. I lay there trying to staunch the bleeding when an almighty explosion sent Sergeant Atkins flying into the same crater.

**Hargreaves** So in the middle of a battle you decide to become friends?

**Atkins** Not quite like that, sir.

**Schmitt** No, not at all like that, Harry. You probably have not yet experienced it, but a high explosive detonating very close to you plays the devil with your senses. You can't hear, speak, or balance. Sergeant Atkins had just been blown up, his knee was dislocated and he was bleeding heavily from a thigh wound. And do you know what he did as soon as his brain stopped rattling around in his skull?

**Hargreaves** No.

**Schmitt** He tried to attack me. Oh he had no weapons, in fact he had very little clothing, but he still struggled up on his one good leg and spraying blood he advanced with the only weapon he had to hand.

**Hargreaves** Which was?

**Schmitt** His commanding officer's leg.

**Hargreaves** Good God, man! What did you do?

**Schmitt** I think mild hysteria must have set in – remember I too was concussed and bleeding. Well when you see a man fly through the air naked apart from his putties and jacket who then wobbles to his feet brandishing a third leg at you, what else is there to do, but laugh?

**Hargreaves** You laughed.

**Schmitt** Oh *ja*, I thought I was going to die, but still the sight of Tommy standing there with a spare leg, which incidentally looked better than either of his own, it was just too much. I laughed and laughed until I started to cry.

**Atkins** Hard to kill a man when he's wetting himself laughing, sir.

**Hargreaves** I can imagine. Then what did you both do?

**Schmitt** Well, Tommy started to laugh as well, just before he fainted. I then reset his knee and bound his wound up with the putties I took from Captain Jennings' leg. I suppose I could have taken advantage of the situation — after all I now had the leg — but somehow it didn't seem, how do you say, ah — chivalrous, to club an unconscious man to death.

**Atkins** When I came round the barrage had stopped. Neither of us fancied sticking our head out of the shell hole, so we started talking. Willy speaks pretty good English, he told me about his time in Blighty, holidays down on the South Coast. He's got a cousin down there.

**Schmitt** And Tommy told me about his family back in Croydon. We also discovered that we had shared many battles. We have both been here since 1914.

**Atkins** It's funny, but when you talk straight to another bloke it's different. Willy stopped being a nun-raping Hun, and became just another poor sod shot full of holes lying in the mud. In what was left of my battledress I had two Woodbines, but no Lucifers.

**Schmitt** And I had a lighter. So we call a truce and have a smoke.

**Hargreaves** Like the football game on Christmas morning — we heard about that at home.

**Rawlings** I was there.

**Hargreaves** Really, Corporal?

**Cpl Rawlings** Yes, sir. Christmas morning, St Yvon, 1914. We sang carols, then walked out into no-man's-land, shared some schnapps, a bit of food and a fag. Kicked a ball about for ten minutes, then we was ordered back into our own lines. Officer told me it was fraternizing with the enemy, and if it happened again he'd have us all shot. But those Germans were all right. They were just like us.

**Hargreaves** This appears to be more than just a game of football, though, gentlemen.

**Schmitt** Far better. But let us finish. Tommy had stopped bleeding and his knee was back in, but he could not walk. He had also lost a lot of blood.

**Hargreaves** So what did you do?

**Schmitt** The only thing I could do, I carried him back to our trench.

**Hargreaves** A prisoner, then.

**Atkins** No, sir, I was a guest. My wounds were treated; I was fed. They even gave me a uniform. I was there for ten days. Got to know Willy's lot. There were only twenty-three of them then. Some spoke English, but mostly I talked through Willy.

**Schmitt** We have a lot of respect for men who have been at the Front as long as Tommy has. We are brothers in arms. Then one night we all have a little too much schnapps and the unthinkable happens.

**Hargreaves** This isn't going to be beastly is it?

**Schmitt** Worse. We admitted to each other we didn't want to fight any more. Four years we have been here, and for what?

**Hargreaves** To do your duty, man.

**Rawlings** The war's over, Lieutenant, all bar the paperwork. We just decided we weren't going to die in the last few weeks.

**Hargreaves** So how did you get back to your own lines, Sergeant?

**Atkins** When I could walk, we went out and got a British uniform for Willy. Then I came back in under a flag of truce with him. It was a bit nerve-wracking, so I taught him some music hall songs to sing as we came in, and, well it worked. I shouted out for Corporal Rawlings — course they thought I'd been killed — and, well, it was quite a reunion.

**Schmitt** Then we outlined our plan. We had twenty-two men. You had seventeen. We decided to choose life. The function of both units was to direct artillery fire, estimate enemy losses, carry out skirmish attacks and defend our line.

**Atkins** So we both give co-ordinates for the artillery that will land behind us.

**Rawlings** We send in details of scores of dead Jerries.

**Schmitt** We fire many rounds of ammunition in the air.

**Atkins** And share our rations.

**Schmitt** There is a collection of uniforms in the ruined farmhouse, so we can walk in no-man's-land without arousing suspicion from aircraft.

**Hargreaves** But that's treason. You all took an oath to serve.

**Rawlings** Well, sir, when it comes down to it, it's either words or people. The German soldiers we know aren't quite like we was told, sir. They don't rape nuns or eat dead babies.

**Schmitt** No more than you sodomise choirboys, Harry.

**Hargreaves** Oh dear God.

**Atkins** It's called propaganda sir.

**Schmitt** We have not been without loss up here, Harry. Two days ago your artillery sent a ranging volley in too long. It killed six of us, three from each side. There was no point. They were not trying to take another few yards of this dead soil, or rescue fallen comrades, they were playing cards.

**Rawlings** Private Bradley was just seventeen. Do you know what the poor sod was most frightened of? He didn't want to go for a Burton before he got his end away. I suppose that's treason as well.

**Hargreaves** I understand how you all must feel, but you must know mutineers can never win. You simply cannot do this. What would happen if every soldier thought like you do?

**Rawlings** Then they might settle things with diplomacy, sir. And nine million souls might not be rotting in the mud.

**Schmitt** Is it so bad what we do, Harry?

*Hargreaves jumps forward, knocks down Schmitt and snatches up his own pistol*

**Hargreaves** Don't you see, I can't let you get away with this. That would make everything I believe in wrong. I have waited all my life to serve and I'm not giving that up to a raggle taggle company of mutineers. Right, last chance. Sergeant Atkins, you will assemble the entire company and tell them they are marching back with me now.

**Rawlings** No, hold on.

**Hargreaves** Shut up, Corporal, I haven't killed anybody yet, but I am perfectly willing to start with you if you utter one more word.

**Atkins** I'm not marching our last fourteen men back to face a firing squad, sir.

**Hargreaves** Very well. I shall return alone, and I will kill anybody that tries to stop me. God help you all when I report to HQ.

**Rawlings** But, sir!

**Hargreaves** I warned you. (*He cocks the pistol*)

**Atkins** Easy, sir, the corporal isn't going to say another word. Are you, Corporal Rawlings?

**Rawlings** No, Sarge.

*Hargreaves takes Schmitt's pistol, then backs away, pointing his gun as he exits*

**Schmitt** Now, quickly, you must come to our line. We will work out some way to hide you.

**Rawlings** No need for that, Willy.

**Schmitt** But he will be back in the British trenches in twenty minutes.

**Atkins** What time is it, Dave?

**Rawlings** Half-past eleven.

*Sounds of heavy artillery and flashes of light outside the dugout, indicating gunfire*

*There is a long pause*

**Atkins** No he won't.

**Rawlings** Poor bastard, he didn't have a clue did he?

**Atkins** Better prepare a report for HQ about Lieutenant Hargreaves.

**Schmitt** May I suggest an epitaph of "greater love has no man than this, than to lay down his life for his friends".

**Rawlings** It would look good for his family, Sarge.

*Sgt Atkins pours three drinks*

**Sgt Atkins** Lieutenant Hargreaves; *Dulce et Decorum est.*

*All drink, then stand to attention, heads bowed*

*The Last Post is played*

CURTAIN

# FURNITURE AND PROPERTY LIST

*On stage*: A table *On it*: a field phone, three tin mugs, some papers, an ashtray, a box of Swan Vesta matches and a packet of Woodbines
Two chairs
Map pinned to wall
Piece of paper with list of names, many crossed out, pinned to wall
Saucy picture of a 1918 starlet, pinned to wall

*Offstage:* Two mugs of tea, twice (**Rawlings**)
A bottle of alcohol and a large German sausage (**Schmitt**)

*Personal*: **Hargreaves**: letter, gun
**Schmitt:** gun

## FIREARMS AND OTHER WEAPONS USED IN THEATRE PRODUCTIONS

With regards to the rules and regulations of firearms and other weapons used in theatre productions, we recommend that you read the Entertainment Information Sheet No. 20 (Health and Safety Executive).

This information sheet is one of a series produced in consultation with the Joint Advisory Committee for Broadcasting and the Performing Arts. It gives guidance on the management of weapons that are part of a production, including firearms, replicas and deactivated weapons.

This sheet may be downloaded from: www.hse.gov.uk. Alternatively, you can contact HSE Books, P O Box 1999, Sudbury, Suffolk, CO10 2WA Tel: 01787 881165 Fax: 01787 313995.

# LIGHTING PLOT

Practicals required: nil
Interior. The same scene throughout

*To open*: Dim lighting

| | | |
|---|---|---|
| *Cue* 1 | **Cpl Rawlings**: "Half-past eleven."<br>*Lights flash outside the dugout to indicate gunfire* | (Page 14) |

# EFFECTS PLOT

| | | |
|---|---|---|
| *Cue* 1 | Curtain rises<br>*Music: It's a Long Way to Tipperary fades out* | (Page 1) |
| *Cue* 2 | **Cpl Rawlings**: "Half-past eleven."<br>*Sound of heavy artillery* | (Page 15) |
| *Cue* 3 | **Cpl Rawlings**, **Sgt Atkins** and **Lt Schmitt** stand, heads bowed<br>*Music: The Last Post* | (Page 15) |

# MUSIC COPYRIGHT

A licence issued by Samuel French Ltd to perform this play does not include permission to use the Incidental music specified in this copy. Where the place of performance is already licensed by the Performing Right Society a return of the music used must be made to them. If the place of performance is not so licensed then application should be made to the Performing Right Society, 29 Berners Street, London W1T 3AB (website: www.mcps-prs-alliance.co.uk).

A separate and additional licence from Phonographic Performance Ltd, 1 Upper James Street, London W1F 9DE (website: www.ppluk.com) is needed whenever commercial recordings are used.

www.ingramcontent.com/pod-product-compliance
Lightning Source LLC
Chambersburg PA
CBHW070456050426
42450CB00012B/3301